"*40 Weeks of Nurture* is a great resource to any mother-to-be who desires to impact the life of her unborn baby from conception to delivery. Foundation is everything! These scriptural confessions for forty weeks over the baby will build a solid foundation for the life of the child you are carrying and also strengthen your faith against any fiery darts the Enemy may throw at you. Hallelujah! I strongly endorse this book!"

—**Pastor Ruth Okiomah**
Founder of Precious Cedars Mother Care, Head of Department, Miracle Mothers Ministry, Living Word Chapel, Houston, Texas

"Tolu Olumuyiwa has written a timeless piece that really helps every mother to connect with her baby in a special and unique way from conception to childbirth and beyond. Every mother deserves to read this."

—**Chiddy Carter**
Singer, Songwriter, Founder and CEO Guitarlina School of Music

"Wow! Tolu really hit the nail on the head with this one. She has given the world an insight into how to turn negativity into positivity. A way to begin well and finish well. Whatever your own story of pregnancy is, this book has a lot to offer. A must read for all!"

—**Pastor Bukky Oisaghie**
Christ Embassy Church, East Bay, California

40 WEEKS OF
NURTURE

Tolu Olumuyiwa

40 Weeks of Nurture
Copyright 2018 by Tolu Olumuyiwa

All rights reserved. No part of this book may be reproduced, stored in a retrieval system, or transmitted in any form or by any means-electronic, mechanical, photocopy, recording, or otherwise-without prior written permission of the copyright owner.

All Scripture references were paraphrased using the *Holy Bible, New Living Translation*, copyright © ©1996, 2004, 2007, 2013, 2015 by Tyndale House Foundation. Used by permission of Tyndale House Publishers Inc., Carol Stream, Illinois 60188. All rights reserved.

This book is dedicated to women trusting God to conceive and bear their own children. Hold steadfast to God; His promises are true. You will bring forth your own child in due season. And to the women who desire to raise godly children in today's noisy world, there are enough of us to make a difference.

Acknowledgments

To my husband, Ibukun: You allow me to fly.

Our children, Great and Goldie: You are the joys of my life. I am committed to giving you my best self.

My sisters, Seyi, Kemi, and Oore: You continue to nurture me.

My parents: For everything.

To the women who have gone ahead of me: I will raise the banner.

Tes and Chiddy: For helping me edit the manuscript and sharing so many cool ideas.

Contents

How to Read This book	11
Foreword	13
Letter to Mothers	15
Preface	17

Section 1: Core — 21

Week 1: Worth	23
Week 2: Sincere	24
Week 3: Kind	25
Week 4: Beautiful	26
Week 5: Honor	27
Week 6: Pure	28
Week 7: Grace	29
Week 8: Treasure	30
Week 9: Love	31

Section 2: Personality Traits — 33

Week 10: Giver	35
Week 11: Joyful	36
Week 12: Wisdom	37
Week 13: Knowledge	38
Week 14: Winner	39
Week 15: Understanding	40

Section 3: Leadership Attributes — 41

Week 16: Leader	43
Week 17: Diligent	44
Week 18: Astute	45
Week 19: Studious	46

Week 20: Greatness — 47
Week 21: Courage — 48

Section 4: Spirituality — 49

Week 22: Worship — 51
Week 23: Peace — 52
Week 24: Divinity — 53
Week 25: Wealth — 54
Week 26: Compassion — 55
Week 27: Blessing — 56
Week 28: Health — 57
Week 29: Thankful — 58
Week 30: Counsel — 59
Week 31: Victor — 60
Week 32: Spiritual — 61
Week 33: Prayerful — 62
Week 34: Power — 63

Section 5: Relationships — 65

Week 35: Discernment — 67
Week 36: Friend — 68
Week 37: Child — 69
Week 38: Sibling — 70
Week 39: Spouse — 71
Week 40: Parent — 72
Epilogue — 73
Take the Charge! — 75

How to Read This book

There are many desires, hopes, and dreams that every parent has for their child. I have shared some of mine here. Each week, I share a synopsis of the topic. In addition to my summary, you can elaborate by adding your special desires for your individual child. I recommend that you write your thoughts in the extra space left for you each week. The book is sectioned into five parts, and each section has an overall theme. This is by no means an exhaustive list. My desire is to give you a starting point and encourage you to be intentional during your pregnancy and throughout your child's nurturing years.

I am deeply grateful that you have committed to reading my book. Please take the pledge at the end.

Enjoy!

Tolu Olumuyiwa

Foreword

On the day I met Tolu—the author of *40 Weeks of Nurture*—the Frankfurt Airport was not one of typical German efficiency. It was instead filled with crowds stranded by massive flight delays. The waiting areas, lounges, and restaurants were overflowing with tired and irritated travelers. My husband and I finally found an empty bench in a café where we could sit and wait for our new flight time to be announced.

As we sipped our lattes, we noticed a weary, pregnant woman pushing a stroller with a sleeping boy. She was looking for a place in the crowd to sit for a while, somewhere to rest her tired body and mind from hours of traveling, but there were no vacant seats anywhere in the airport. We invited her and her little one to share our bench with us. We had no idea that this seemingly chance encounter was actually a divine appointment that would be the beginning of a cherished friendship.

It was a fitting first meeting. Tolu reminded us of another weary traveling pregnant woman: Mary, the mother of Jesus. She, too, was searching for a quiet place to rest her tired body. It is this same universal mother's heart that inspired Tolu to write this book for those expecting. She understands the hopes, dreams, fears, and concerns of women everywhere who are carrying a new, precious life inside. She knows the importance of those 40 weeks leading up to the birth of an anticipated child.

40 Weeks of Nurture is like receiving a personal letter from a dear friend guiding you to see God's promises for your baby and helping you to confess God's best for your unborn child's life. As your baby develops physically, you can pray for the soul and character of your child to take form in beautifully strong, healthy ways.

Within your womb is a miracle that bears the fingerprint and image of a loving and caring God. In your belly, an eternal creation is being formed. Your unborn child can feel, hear, and experience more than we imagine while still in its protective cocoon. Sing to your baby. Talk to her. Pray over him. Bless them.

My friend, Tolu, will show you how to do this. *40 Weeks of Nurture* will become a journal and legacy recording your hopes, dreams, and prayers for your child. Someday you will be able to place this very book, filled with your personal thoughts and notes, into your child's hands as a keepsake and reminder of your love and desires for them from conception.

May God bless you and your baby as you make this journey together!

Lynn Jarman
Wife and Mother, Church Planting Coach: The New Life Network
Church Multiplication Catalyst: Converge Worldwide
Strategic Partners Team: ReachGlobal Europe

Letter to Mothers

Dear New Mother,

You have been blessed with the most beautiful gift in the world—the gift of a child. With this gift comes the responsibility of nurture. This book is my challenge for you to start now to influence the holistic person your child will grow up to be.

40 Weeks of Nurture provides every mother with a weekly guide of character traits to pray over her unborn child. Take the traits seriously when you speak them over your baby and believe them. Create a picture of your child, developing the character traits that will be discussed within the book.

The tongue, of its own, is mighty in the way it facilitates the intake of nutrients into the body. It can also communicate power to your unborn child. When you speak words, imagine that these words are nutrients that you are feeding your child. When you pray certain character traits over your child, you are nourishing your child's mind with nutrients. Use your tongue as a creative compass to chart the course of your child's life.

Over forty weeks, I documented the character traits I desired for my own children. However, I encourage you to use this book as a guide, not an exhaustive list. Write your own notes, personalize it with your child's name and give it as a gift to your child in the future. You can choose to replace some of my character traits with other spiritual, physical, or mental traits you may specifically desire for your child.

Here is how I ingested these nutrients over forty weeks:

Each week I identified a character trait to pray over my child. As soon as I woke up in the morning, I peeked at which nutrient I was feeding the baby that week. When I got into the shower, I uttered words of affirmation and prayed that nutrient over my child. I would share these moments of intimacy with my child for the entire week before moving on to the next nutrient. As I spoke over my child, I imagined them receiving these words and pictured him or her growing into the person I was desiring them to be.

A mother's nurture never ends; it begins as soon as the baby presents itself in the womb, so I encourage you to begin nurturing your baby from the womb. This will have a tremendous impact on the child when he/she is grown. Just as scientific research shows that women who have access to prenatal care have healthier babies, research based on Scripture shows that words have power. The power to create lies in the tongue.

My prayer for you:

> I am confident that you will strategically and intentionally nourish your body physically and spiritually while carrying your baby. As a result, our children will grow up to be spiritual giants with godly character traits. They will be wholesome individuals with healthy minds, bodies, and spirits who will plaster the world with love. Our world needs this now more than ever before.

Preface

Fear is the thief of joy and the enemy of faith.

Both times I was pregnant, I was very afraid. I was sick (especially in my first trimester) and overtaken with fear. I could barely keep any food in my stomach. Crazy thoughts ran through my mind constantly. *What if I died? What if my baby didn't survive because of poor nutrition?* This book was born in that season. I learned during that time that I had power in my mouth, and I could speak life over my unborn child.

This book is dedicated to women everywhere, pregnant and expecting.

I want to remind you your words have power. Amidst telling your mate and freaking out because it finally happened, the first thing most women do when they get pregnant is visit the doctor. The doctor then recommends that the woman take prenatal vitamins, or supplements. These supplements are supposed to aid the growth and development of the baby. Most women take these vitamins judiciously for forty weeks. We do so because we want to provide the most nurturing environment for our growing child. But what if you are unable to take pills or vitamins or anything for that matter? Where does your body get the nutrients it needs to nurture the baby then?

That was the case for me. My body was failing and I had to completely rely on my spirit to live. Even my mind couldn't really focus. I could not eat or take any medications. Everything that went into my mouth inevitably came back out the same way it had entered. I was consumed by a variety of thoughts—some plausible, like, *What if my baby doesn't get enough nutrients causing it not to survive?* Others were wildly unfounded: *What if I just faint and never wake up?* Although at the time these seemed entirely within the realm of possibility. Paradoxically, in my spirit, I was perfectly fine. When I could, I would encourage my body by speaking words from my spirit; and in that moment, I would feel better. I realized that if I could speak to myself and get better, then I could also speak to my baby. I could speak to my baby because I had power in my words and my body was responding to those words.

I thought, *God has given me the gift of a child, so I have the responsibility to take care of him or her.* I started processing this deeply and engaging my mind. I found solace in knowing that if physicians with their human minds could prescribe medications and they worked most of the time, then God who I believe is the embodiment of wisdom must have a way for me. Surely, He must have a way to take care of the child in the uterus. I wanted my baby to be healthy and I was too sick to take medications, so I decided to feed on the Word of God as my medicine. I started professing that my baby was healthy. I came up with a plan—I would speak specific Scriptures repeatedly to my body and imagine they were medicine. If God had said it, I believed it. I treated Scripture as my medication and took this medication week after week. As I consistently spoke God's Word, I felt a very powerful connection begin to develop between my baby and me. As time progressed, the fear disappeared and I started to have faith in my confessions. I was becoming less worried. I realized the health of my child was not in the hands of some pills but in the power of my words, God's promises to me. God had trusted me with this baby and everything I needed was inside me. This experience grew my faith, but it wasn't always easy.

Around the same time, I started to wonder how the mind of a child was shaped. Medical science is very focused on the physical development of the human body, but I know there is much more to a child's development than that.

The mind and spirit are equally as important as the body. The mind is the seat of intellect; the spirit is who a person inherently is. The spirit of God started to reveal more about this to me. God cares about the person a child develops into. God started to show me how much power I had over my unborn child and how I could use my words to begin to mold the mind of my child. I was excited about this new discovery. Every week I picked a character or personality trait and prayed it over my child. For example, if I chose confidence for that week, I placed my hand on my stomach and just spoke to my baby, praying that he or she would be confident. This was very empowering and eased away fear. I began documenting what I was saying, and that is how this book was born. As I wrote and I proclaimed God's Word, I figured it would be easier if a pregnant woman had the affirmations already written out as a guide. All she would have to do was speak them to her baby.

I have written forty character traits to help you connect and pray with your baby. Each trait can be the focus for a week and prayed over your baby each day of that week. Use this as a workbook; personalize it by writing your baby's name and specific traits unique to your child; then, sometime in the future, present it as a gift to your child. This list of character traits is not exhaustive as each of our desires for our children are different. I left a few blank lines for you in each chapter so you can personalize it.

As you speak these words, your soul will be nurtured. The spoken words will echo back to you as a reminder of the need to be nurtured yourself.

Section 1: Core

At your core, know your worth; be sincere and kind. Remember grace will bring you through. Honor everyone. Stay pure; discover the beauty and treasure within you, and always be full of love and abide in God's love.

Week 1: Worth

You are my prize, my fair share, my portion. I knew you before you were born.

(See Jeremiah 1:5.)

Know your worth. You are prized above all else. God placed this value upon you when He made you. Never allow the world to place its own value on you. Always remember that your worth shall not depreciate, even though not everyone will agree. Your worth may sometimes be underestimated, but never worry about that.

The real prize is that you know your worth, especially when everyone else around you cannot see it or recognize it. This understanding will be rooted and grounded in you. You will recognize this about yourself and teach others the value of prizing themselves in Christ.

Action: Place your hand on your growing stomach and say to your baby:

> "Child, you are highly valued. Only your heavenly Father completely comprehends your value and worth. You will be strongly convicted of this truth and convinced that Jesus Christ paid the ultimate price for you. Never devalue yourself."

Week 2: Sincere

Be truthful, sincere, and loyal.
(See Proverbs 3:3.)

You will be a sincere child. Mean what you say, and say what you mean. Be sincere in your words and actions and let no craftiness or deceit be found in you. You will be known for honesty and truth, for God honors these things. You will confidently stand up for the things you believe in. Your words will be seasoned and graced always.

When you speak, your words will be genuine and heartfelt. I look forward to interacting with you and watching you grow into all these things.

Action: Write a personal note to your child here; describe the benefits of being honest and sincere.

_____

_____

_____

_____

_____

_____

Section 1: Core

Week 3: Kind

Be kind, show kindness always!
(See Ephesians 4:32.)

Kindness is a rare commodity these days. I pray you are kind, compassionate, warm-hearted, and considerate. Kindness is a fruit of the Spirit and compassion is expected of you as a child of God. You are compassionate, always willing to listen and lend a hand. God will be kind toward you and you will extend this kindness to others, just as Jesus was kind to all. He is your role model, so be kind. You will have a warm heart; you'll be concerned about and compassionate toward others.

Action: Write a personal note to your child here. Share the rewards of being kind and compassionate.

_____

_____

_____

_____

_____

_____

_____

_____

Week 4: Beautiful

God made you beautiful and named you wonderful.
(See Psalm 139:14.)

Never forget this, because the world will try to tell you otherwise. God took His time to mold you, and He perfected all that concerns you. Remember that beauty is not only external. True beauty lies on the inside, not the outside.

Action: Place your hand over your womb and say to your baby:

> "I pray you are never bothered when someone tells you something that contradicts God's promises to you. Remember you hail from above and God made you perfectly in heaven."

Section 1: Core

Week 5: Honor

Honor everyone, love people, love God.
(See 1 Peter 2:17.)

And whatever you find yourself doing, do it with all your heart as an honor to yourself. Have reverence for God and honor everyone.

Action: Place your hand over your womb and say to your baby:

"I pray that you are a child of honor and remember this when people deal unkindly with you. Always take the high road and honor everyone."

Week 6: Pure

You can easily hear God's voice when you have a pure heart.
(See Matthew 5:8.)

Stay pure for Jesus. Guard your heart with seriousness of purpose because the state of your heart determines the quality of your life. Don't feel pressured to expose your heart to something or someone your spirit is uncomfortable with. Your definition of purity might differ from the world's definition, but that is acceptable.

Action: Write a personalized note to your child. Share your thoughts on purity and encourage your child to live a pure, holy, and undefiled life.

_____
_____
_____
_____
_____
_____
_____
_____

Section 1: Core

Week 7: Grace

God's grace is available to the humble.
(See James 4:6.)

There is an unmistakable grace about you. God's grace makes challenges bearable and reminds you that you don't have to struggle alone in life. I pray you never forget this profound truth. I pray you are described as gracious. Always be full of grace, putting others ahead of yourself. Once you understand what it means to be graced by God, it will be easy for you to be gracious. Speak this truth to yourself always.

Action: Place your hand over your womb and say to your baby:

> "I pray the grace of our Lord Jesus Christ, the love of God, and the fellowship of the Holy Spirit be with you forever."

Week 8: Treasure

You are a treasure wrapped in skin; you reveal God's greatness.
(See 2 Corinthians 4:7.)

No one ever woke up and found a treasure lying carelessly beside them. A treasure is usually dug out. When found, it is valued as precious stone. You, my child, are a treasure. As you grow up, you will learn the value of digging deep inside to uncover the treasure that you are. As you do this, I pray you grow in the understanding of your purpose.

Action: Place your hand over your womb and say to your baby:

> "I pray you are reminded that you are a treasure.
> God wrapped up His excellence in you. Invest time
> in unlocking the depth of the greatness that lies
> inside you."

Section 1: Core

Week 9: Love

Let love and faithfulness be part of your core.
(See Proverbs 3:3.)

Love is in your nature. You will understand what it is to love and be loved. God's love is the purest and most undiluted form of love. Seek to find love in people who first love God. Anyone who does not love God cannot love you. How can a person say *I love you* if they cannot love God, their Creator?

Love is powerful; it is of God. If you find it difficult to love a person, try to see the person from the lens through which God sees them. Remember that love does not keep a record of wrongs. Read more from 1 Corinthians 13.

Action: Place your hand over your womb and say to your baby:

> "You'll always love God who first loved you and you'll love all God's creation. I pray you love your neighbor as you do yourself."

Section 2: Personality Traits

Your personality shines through your giving and joyful nature, your application of knowledge and wisdom, your willingness to understand life's circumstances and seasons, and overall, your winning attitude. Let these things shine through you.

Week 10: Giver

You are more blessed when you give than when you receive.
(See Acts 20:35.)

You have freely received the blessing of life. In the same way, freely give of your love, your time, and your very self. We give because God first gave us His Son, Jesus. There will always be people in the world who don't have as much as you do; reach out to them. When you give to the poor and needy, you are lending to God.

Action: Place your hand on your womb and say to your baby:

> "I pray you have a mindset that is generous and readily gives."

Write a note to your child sharing a testimony of the blessing of giving. Hopefully, your child can refer to your note when he or she finds giving challenging.

_____

_____

_____

_____

_____

Week 11: Joyful

Be happy; find your strength in God's joy.
(See Nehemiah 8:10.)

I pray that your joy flows like a river and that you will let nothing steal your joy. Joy is a fruit of God's Spirit. When sad moments come, don't linger in those moments for too long. Stand in front of a mirror and say, "My name is Joy." Sing your favorite song. If you are too sad to sing, play a happy tune and keep joyful music around you all the time.

Action: Place your hand over your womb and say to your baby:

> "I pray you learn to call forth joy when it seems absent. May you always be full of joy and infuse your life with a joyful spirit."

Section 2: Personality Traits

Week 12: Wisdom

By all means, get wisdom.
(See Proverbs 4:7.)

You will be wise, discerning, and of good judgment. Wisdom is paramount in making the right choices and decisions in life.

Action: Place your hand over your womb and say to your baby:

> "I pray you seek God always, for He is the embodiment of all wisdom. Discernment is given by the Holy Spirit. Listen for His voice, and then you will make wise decisions. You will listen to godly counsel and accept instruction. You will be counted among the wise. When you lack wisdom, ask God. He gives freely." Read James 1:5.

A Special Note about Wisdom:

My husband was sixteen years old when he arrived in the United States to attend college. He felt as though he had been thrown into an ocean and left to swim among sharks. He realized early that he was young and lacked the sagacity to navigate his new environment. He quickly metamorphosed from being the top graduating high school student of his year in his home country to an unremarkable, average student. One day, he asked God for wisdom simply by professing James 1:5, which says that if anyone lacks wisdom, let him ask and it will be given to him. Hence, by simply asking God for wisdom, he watched himself grow in wisdom. My husband remains one of the smartest people I know.

40 Weeks of Nurture

Week 13: Knowledge

Cultivate a curious and an open mind, always willing to learn.
(See Proverbs 15:14.)

I pray you have a sensitive spirit. You will seek knowledge and you will find it. Apply yourself, and thirst for knowledge. The more you learn, the more you'll want to learn. Everything you need to know in life, you will learn through God's Spirit.

Action: Place your hand over your womb and say to your baby:

> "I pray God teaches you knowledge and good judgment."

Section 2: Personality Traits

Week 14: Winner

After you have received Christ, you will reign and rule in this life.
(See Romans 5:17.)

You will develop and have the mindset of a winner. Remember the Scripture that says in all these things you are more than a conqueror (Romans 8:37). Nothing can defeat you or cause you to fail in this life. And remember, your failure at anything does not mean you are a loser. You will always be a winner because your God has made you so. Winners seize opportunities. If you fall seven times, then stand up again seven times. Winning is an attribute you must cultivate.

Action: Place your hand over your womb and say to your baby:

> "I pray you develop the mindset of a winner. May you always be ready to stand up when you fall."

Week 15: Understanding

Teach me to stay focused.
(See Proverbs 4:25.)

You will understand your purpose and have a clear vision. You have the Spirit of understanding at work in you. I pray you will always try to understand the times and seasons of your life. This means you will not measure your life by the decisions others make for you or compare yourself to your peers. You are specially made by God, and He has plans for you that others have no knowledge about. You will understand what season you are in and function in that season.

Action: Place your hand over your womb and say to your baby:

> "You have the spirit of understanding. Whenever you are in doubt, remember to ask for help from God your Father who freely gives us all things. Seek to understand people and to tolerate and appreciate differing viewpoints."

Section 3: Leadership Attributes

A leader is diligent, astute, courageous, studious, and exudes greatness. I pray you grow into a visionary and exemplary leader and that these attributes are a part of you.

Week 16: Leader

Anyone who wants to be first must be the very last, and the servant of all
(See Mark 9:35.)

A leader can wear the hats of both teacher and servant and is prepared at all times. Be a leader like Jesus. Be willing to receive counsel. Be ready to serve. One of the disciples of Jesus, Mark, records that Jesus called His twelve disciples and said to them, "Anyone who wants to be first must be the very last, and the servant of all."

Action: Write your personal thoughts on leadership for your child.

_____

_____

_____

_____

_____

_____

_____

Week 17: Diligent

A diligent man will stand before kings.
(See Proverbs 22:29.)

Diligence requires hard work and consistency. Diligence is required of a leader. Go the extra mile, work hard, and be consistent. I pray you develop this skill early in life. If you do, you will go very far and be exceptional.

Action: Place your hand over your womb and say to your baby:

> "I pray you have the spirit of diligence and skill. I pray your diligence and skill make way for you."

Section 3: Leadership Attributes

Week 18: Astute

Trust God; lean not on your own understanding.
(See Proverbs 3:5.)

It is important to understand and develop human relationships. However, it is more important to trust and depend on God's Spirit for a roadmap for navigating human relationships. To be successful at this, you need to be able to assess situations and people. You need to know when to give a hug and when to extend a handshake; to know when to run in and when to walk away.

Action: Place your hand over your womb and say to your baby:

> "I pray you are clever, sharp-minded, and quick of understanding. I pray you will wholeheartedly rely on God."

Week 19: Studious

Study so you can be approved by God.
(See 2 Timothy 2:15b.)

I pray you develop a love for books and a passion for studying. The more you study, the further you will go in life. The wisdom of the ages is buried in books, so invest in seeking knowledge. Remember the Bible states that people perish because they lack knowledge. (See Hosea 4:6.) You are born in a time when reading has become a chore instead of a necessary skill that everyone should develop. Cultivate this habit. Be disciplined enough to read a book and patient enough to follow through. Do not only read; write your own book. Pay it forward. People will be happy to read your work.

Action: Write a note to your child; share the benefits you have reaped from studying.

Section 3: Leadership Attributes

Week 20: Greatness

Before I formed you in the womb, I knew you.
(See Jeremiah 1:5.)

The seed of greatness is Christ in you. You come from a lineage of great men and women as the Bible describes. God has blessed you with gifts and talents; therefore, surround yourself with great minds who share the same or higher values as you do. They will inspire you to greatness. I pray you live a life that inspires our world and your gifts and talents honor our God. You will leave indelible marks on the sands of time.

Action: Write in your words what it means to be great and why you aspire for your child to be great.

_____

_____

_____

_____

_____

_____

_____

Week 21: Courage

I have commanded you to be strong and courageous.
(See Joshua 1:9.)

The Bible teaches us to be bold and courageous. Never be afraid to step out of your comfort zone. Be the "yes" person when everyone around you says "no." Do not be afraid to take risks, set sail, and fly. You will take leaps of faith and disavow fear.

Action: Place your hand over your womb and say to your baby:

"I pray you are imbued with boldness and courage."

Section 4: Spirituality

Spirituality is linked to morality, but more than that it is who we are and what we can do with God living inside of us. It is expressed though prayer, counsel, compassion, wealth, peace, power, worship, victory, and blessing our world.

Week 22: Worship

God is Spirit, so our worship must be done in spirit and truth.
(See John 4:24.)

I pray you live your life in such a way that is pleasing to God, and that you will understand what it means to connect with the Spirit of God. As a child, you will lift your hands in worship to God all your days. Everything about you will worship God. You will lead many in worship and inspire many to worship. You will be as a sweet-smelling savor unto God.

Action: Place your hand over your womb and say to your baby:

"You will worship God in reverence and awe."

Week 23: Peace

My peace I give to you.
(See John 14:27.)

God has given you peace. This peace is unexplainable. Enjoy this gift of peace and let nothing trouble you. As much as you can, pursue peace with everyone and never repay evil with evil.

Action: Place your hand over your womb and say to your baby:

> "I pray you learn to rest in God. I pray you seek peace always and stay out of trouble. Above all, may you be a peacemaker."

Section 4: Spirituality

Week 24: Divinity

I will leave my Spirit with you.
(See John 14:16.)

You are made in the image and likeness of God. Divinity is at work in you. This simply means you are not an ordinary child. God lives on the inside of you. When Jesus left the earth, He left His Spirit with you and He will abide in you forever. When you have absorbed this truth, you will live your life as someone whose bodyguard is God.

Action: Place your hand over your womb and say to your baby:

> "God's Spirit lives inside of you. You are a God-carrier. Have this mindset always."

Week 25: Wealth

God will provide all that you need.
(See Philippians 4:19.)

God has given you the power to make wealth, so make wealth. I pray you live in abundance. You will have a mindset and a belief that all your sufficiency is in God. Remember God's promise to Abraham: God made Abraham the father of many nations and made him wealthy. You are the seed of Abraham; therefore, you are born into wealth. You are wealthy! You are a giver to the nations of the world. You will master the art of money management; money will be a slave to you. It is true that money is a defense, but remember it is God our Father who gives us power to create wealth. He is the Monarch of the Universe.

Action: Write a note to your child explaining what true wealth means to you.

_____

_____

_____

_____

_____

Section 4: Spirituality

Week 26: Compassion

When Jesus looked at them, He had compassion.
(See Matthew 9:36.)

You are growing up to be a loving and compassionate soul. Your heart will never wax cold. You will have a heart that is sensitive to the plight of others and offer a helping hand when you can. Like Jesus, you will be moved with compassion to offer help to those suffering or hurting around you.

Action: Place your hand over your womb and say to your baby:

"I pray you are always full of compassion and quick to help those in need."

Week 27: Blessing

I will bless those who bless you and curse those who treat you with contempt.

(See Genesis 12:3.)

When God has blessed you, you cannot be cursed. You are blessed, and God has made you a blessing to others. Remember this, especially when people say negative things about you or try to curse you. Their words have no power, so never let them get beneath your skin. God has blessed you and no negative word spoken concerning you can ever come to pass. Make sure you are a blessing to others.

Action: Place your hand over your womb and say to your baby:

"You are born to be blessed and to be a blessing."

Section 4: Spirituality

Week 28: Health

By His stripes, we were healed.
(See Isaiah 53:5.)

The reference above is written in past tense and refers to something that already happened. If you find yourself sick, remember this Scripture and confess that you are healthy and strong. You have the DNA of God's Spirit; therefore, no disease or sickness can fasten itself to your body. If you ever find yourself sick in your body, rebuke sickness and simply say, "I am healed by God." Believe this truth.

Action: Write a note to your child documenting a time when you were sick and God healed you. This will be a testimony of the power of God to heal and a reminder to your child to trust God in, and against, sickness.

_____

_____

_____

_____

_____

_____

_____

Week 29: Thankful

Let everything that breathes praise the Lord!
(See Psalms 150:6.)

Be thankful in all things and in all seasons. God loves a grateful heart. When you are thankful for the things you have, you stop focusing on the things you do not have.

Action: Write about some of the benefits you have received from being thankful to demonstrate the power of thanksgiving from your personal experiences.

_____

_____

_____

_____

_____

_____

_____

_____

_____

Section 4: Spirituality

Week 30: Counsel

There is safety in receiving wise counsel
(See Proverbs 11:4.)

The Spirit of Counsel is one of the attributes of the Spirit of God. You have the Spirit of Counsel and you are open to receiving counsel from the Holy Spirit and from those led by God. You are patient enough to give counsel as required of you. When you don't know what to do, seek counsel. I pray you have a teachable spirit.

Action: Place your hand over your womb and say to your baby:

> "It is okay to acknowledge what you do not know and be willing to learn. After you have learned, be willing to teach others. The Holy Spirit is the Spirit of Truth. He will teach you all things. Just ask."

Week 31: Victor

You have victory through Jesus, our Lord!
(See 1 Corinthians 15:57.)

You are victorious in all things through Christ. Victory is yours always because Jesus already paid the price for you. I pray you grow in this knowledge and in this might. You can never be defeated.

Action: Place your hand over your womb and say to your baby:

> "I pray you have the mindset of a victor. Even when you may have lost a fight, do not lose the mindset of a victor. The battle is the Lord's and you are victorious."

Section 4: Spirituality

Week 32: Spiritual

For what is seen is temporary, but what is unseen is forever.
(See 2 Corinthians 4:18.)

Always remember that life is spiritual. When things happen physically and you want to change them, sometimes all that is required from you is to pray about them. Never forget that all things in the physical realm stem from the spiritual. You must learn to trust God for all things and in all things. Keep your gaze on Jesus always.

Action: Place your hand over your womb and say to your baby:

> "There is a God who sits in the heavens and He is your Father. Without Him, nothing was made that exists. Do not get overwhelmed by physical challenges. Remember that the Master of the Universe is your Father. Talk to Him about your issues and learn to relax in His embrace. There are many battles that you will win by simply talking to God about them. If you can take hold of this truth, nothing will phase you physically. You will learn to deal with things from a spiritual point of view, with depth and spiritual insight."

Week 33: Prayerful

Pray always!
(See 1 Thessalonians 5:17.)

Prayer is a sacred need. You will begin praying even before you begin to talk. You will be a praying child, a praying youth, a praying spouse, a praying parent, and a praying friend.

Action: Place your hand over your womb and say to your baby:

> "Every time you pray, your utterances will go from your lips to God's ears. Your prayers will bring about change; they will be filled with faith and offer hope to many. You will experience miracles through prayer and nothing will be impossible unto you. Learn to rest after you have prayed. You will develop the habit of praying very early, and you will hear the voice of God and obey Him all your life."

Section 4: Spirituality

Week 34: Power

And you'll receive power after the Holy Spirit has come upon you.
(See Acts 1:8.)

As a Christian, you have power that is dynamic in the way it works and produces results. There's no limit to what this power can accomplish because it is God's power that is in you. Your thoughts have power; your words have power. Have this mindset and allow it to influence the way you speak and think.

Action: Place your hand over your womb and say to your child:

> "You are powerful. God's power works in you always. I pray you are always conscious of your words and thoughts because God's power in you can bring them to life. This knowledge will put you on top always."

Section 5: Relationships

Your relationships are a thread that will weave your life experiences together. Use discernment in your choices; develop friendships. As a child, honor your parents as you will someday have your own children. Support your siblings, love and honor your spouse, and be a present parent.

Week 35: Discernment

My child, be discerning. Use your God-given sense.
(See Proverbs 3:21.)

Discernment is the ability to have good judgment. It is far easier to discern when you have a relationship with God because you can receive guidance from God's Spirit in you. To develop any relationship at all, you must be able to understand compatibility, acceptance, and purpose.

Action: Place your hand over your womb and say to your baby:

> "I pray you can discern right from wrong, truth from error. This ability will help you choose your friends and grow in the right relationships."

Week 36: Friend

Be a friend who is always there!
(See Proverbs 18:24.)

You will be a friend of God and He will call you friend. You will be a friend in need and a friend in deed, a friend who sticks closer than a brother or sister.

Action: Write a note sharing a friendship story that has been a blessing to you. One that will inspire your child to nurture friendships.

_____

_____

_____

_____

_____

_____

_____

_____

_____

Section 5: Relationships

Week 37: Child

For this child, we prayed and the Lord heard us.
(See 1 Samuel 1:27.)

I dreamed of you before you were born. You are God's perfect gift to us. You are a delight to your parents and a gold standard for a child. Only the workmanship of a Master and the perfection of our God could have given you to me. I pray you grow up to be everyone's dream child. You are first and foremost God's precious possession, made with a heart pure as gold. You are the apple of God's eyes. You will be taught by God and instructed in righteousness. You will be an obedient child. You will love and honor your parents and we will raise you in love. We will be exemplary parents and model what it means to be children by first honoring our parents.

Action: Place your hand over your womb and say to your baby:

> "You will honor your father and mother, and your days on earth will be long, as it says in Ephesians 6:1-3. This is God's commandment."

Week 38: Sibling

Love your brother and sister always
(See Hebrews 13:1.)

Your sibling is your first friend and helper, your confidant and prayer partner. You will love your siblings and be there for each other through life's journey. Above all, I pray you are reminded all the days of your life what a blessing it is for anyone to have you as their sibling.

Action: Write to your baby and include the names of already existing siblings. Include your thoughts on how you desire your children to bond and connect with each other.

Section 5: Relationships

Week 39: Spouse

Helper. Lover. Friend.

(See Song of Solomon 8:4.)

You will not awaken love before it is time. When you find your spouse, you will be pure and chaste, wholly serving God. You will love, honor, and respect your spouse. You will build your home wisely.

Action: Write/share your favorite love story with your child. This will be encouraging when your child is ready to be in a committed relationship.

Week 40: Parent

Train your child in the way they must go.
(See Proverbs 22:6.)

When God gives you a child, remember you were carefully chosen to raise and nurture your child in the way that child is destined to go. I pray, when the time comes, you will raise your children in the way of God, for this is the way that they must go. As a parent, you have a duty to lovingly discipline your children.

Action: Place your hand over your womb and say to your baby:

> "I pray you have all the resources that you need when you become a parent to train up your child in the way of God. May you lead by example."

Epilogue

The relationship between nurture and words is symbiotic; the former is dependent on the latter. The right words spoken can be likened to the right soil for a plant. When a seed is planted in fertile soil, it grows because the law of growth must set forth. Your spoken words can set a note of expectation for who you hope your child will be. By speaking over your baby, you are setting a bar of expectation for your child and developing your nurturing ability. When God gives you an amazing child, He graces you to be able to nurture that child until they attain full maturity in Christ. By nurturing your child, you are in turn nurturing yourself. It is a win-win for you and your child.

You have all that it takes to nurture your child. Pregnancy will stretch you, but childbirth will strengthen you further. *You are built for this journey.* Know this and repeat it when the going gets tough. Refer to this book through the growing years of your child's life and choose carefully the words you speak over your child. According to Scripture, the words we speak have the power to produce results. Words are the seeds we plant in our children. I was stretched during my pregnancies and postpartum seasons, but remembering God's Word and speaking it gave me strength, nourishment, and comfort.

As you nurture your child, speak empowering words to yourself also. Nurturing your mind will create a fertile environment for your baby to grow. If you are going through health challenges or have received an unfavorable diagnosis from your physician, be encouraged. God is greater than the greatest physician and His plans and purposes for you and your child will come to pass. Hold on!

Finally, I want to make a call to every nurturer—dads, moms, grandparents, aunts, uncles, friends, teachers, the entire village! Beyond nurturing our own individual children, I strongly believe that God is calling us to raise a new generation dedicated to serving Him. He is calling us to be intentional about raising children who honor God with their lives and live out their faith intentionally.

I encourage mothers who are not pregnant to take a forty-week journey with this book, intentionally praying over your children. Each book is your connection to the hopes, dreams, and aspirations you have for your child.

For expecting moms and women trusting God to become pregnant, I encourage you to pray these prayers ahead, believing that someday you too would have the opportunity to present this book to your child.

Take the Charge!

If you would, I enjoin you to take this charge with me:

I commit to nurturing my child and other children in this generation using the positive influence of my God-given tongue.

I will speak words that nourish, build up, encourage, guide, bless, and raise the next generation of children, who will raise banners of God's love and be true examples of righteousness.

I will be a godly influence and positive role model for every child I encounter.

I have joined a bandwagon of nurturers, and my prayers make a difference in every little life.

About the Author

Tolu Olumuyiwa is committed to influencing her generation with the love of Jesus. She has taught in children and youth ministry for over fifteen years and is the cofounder of Building This Generation, a nonprofit organization that promotes literacy in children in underserved communities. She is passionate about raising a generation of youth leaders who are Christ-centered and compassionate. She and her husband lead a young adult church in Houston, Texas. They have two beautiful children.

Tolu can be contacted at:
40weeksofnurture@gmail.com

www.ingramcontent.com/pod-product-compliance
Lightning Source LLC
Chambersburg PA
CBHW072106290426
44110CB00014B/1844